Food and Recipes of the Pilgrims

George Erdosh

The Rosen Publishing Group's
PowerKids Press™
New York

The recipes in this cookbook are intended for a child to make together with an adult.

Many thanks to Ruth Rosen and her test kitchen.

Published in 1997 by The Rosen Publishing Group, Inc.
29 East 21st Street, New York, NY 10010

First Edition

Book Design: Danielle Primiceri

Photo Credits: Cover (left) © Corbis-Bettmann, (right) © Scott Barrow/International Stock; pp. 4, 7, 8 (top, middle), 11, 12, 15, 16 (top), 18 (top) © Corbis-Bettmann; p. 20 (top) © Bettmann; p. 20 (middle) Eric A. Wessman/Viesti Associates, Inc.

Photo Illustrations: pp. 8 (middle, bottom), 16 (middle, bottom), 18 (bottom), 20 (bottom) by Ira Fox; pp. 9, 17, 19, 21 by Christine Innamorato and Olga Vega.

Erdosh, George, 1935–
    Food and recipes of the Pilgrims / George Erdosh.
        p.   cm. — (Cooking throughout American history)
    Includes index.
    Summary: Describes the kinds of foods grown and prepared by the Pilgrims during their first years in America, and their dependence upon Native people to ward off starvation. Includes recipes.
    ISBN 0-8239-5117-0
    1. Cookery, American—History—Juvenile literature. 2. Pilgrims (New Plymouth Colony)—Juvenile literature. [1. Cookery, American—History. 2. Pilgrims (New Plymouth Colony).] I. Title. II. Series.
    TX715.E66 1997
    641.59744'09'032—dc21   97-14334
                                                                                                                CIP
                                                                                                                AC

Manufactured in the United States of America

Contents

The English Arrive in America

Benjamin was eight years old when he arrived with his parents in North America in 1620. He was excited, but he was also very hungry. When the boats landed and the 101 **Pilgrims** (PIL-gremz) came ashore, they were almost out of food.

The Pilgrims had been farmers in England, so they knew how to grow food. They had brought seeds with them to plant and grow in their new home. But the seeds didn't grow well in American soil. The Pilgrims soon ran out of the little food they had left.

There were lots of plants and berries on this new land, but the Pilgrims didn't know what was safe to eat. There were wild animals in the forests and fish in the sea, but the Pilgrims didn't know how to hunt or fish. During their first year in North America, the Pilgrims nearly died of **starvation** (star-VAY-shun).

◀ *The Pilgrims landed in what is now Plymouth, Massachusetts.*

Native Americans to the Rescue

The Pilgrims began to think that all was lost. But some friendly Native American Indians, who had lived in North America for hundreds of years, helped the starving Pilgrims. They gave the Pilgrims gifts of corn, meat from wild animals, and fish. Benjamin liked the fish, but not the meat of the wild animals. It took a long time for him to get used to the taste of it.

The Native Americans taught the Pilgrims to hunt and fish. They also taught the Pilgrims to plant corn, a vegetable that the Pilgrims had never seen before. Between the corn stalks, the Indians planted beans and squash. The Pilgrims were amazed to learn how much the Native Americans were able to grow. In the Pilgrims' second year in North America, Benjamin's father **harvested** (HAR-ves-ted) five times more food in North America than he had on the same amount of land in England.

The Native Americans helped the Pilgrims learn how to survive in their new home. ▶

The First Thanksgiving

The new English **settlers** (SET-ul-erz) had a lot to give thanks for after their first good harvest in 1621. To celebrate, they invited their new Native American friends to a great feast. The Pilgrims and Native Americans ate the harvested corn and pumpkins. They also ate wild ducks, geese, turkeys, cornbread, wild plums, nuts, and berries. The weather was mild, and they ate on large tables and benches outside.

Benjamin and the others feasted for three days!

Baked Butternut Squash

You will need:

1 butternut squash
butter
brown sugar

HOW TO DO IT:

☞ Preheat the oven to 400°F.

☞ Cut the butternut squash lengthwise into several pieces.

☞ Cover a baking sheet with aluminum foil and place the squash pieces on top.

☞ Put the baking sheet and the slices of squash in the oven.

☞ Bake for 50 to 60 minutes, or until the squash is brown.

☞ Take it out of the oven and serve it with a little butter and brown sugar sprinkled on top.

You can add to your family's Thanksgiving dinner by making squash the way in which the Pilgrims had learned from the Native Americans.

The First Ten Years

Each year the Pilgrims had more and more food. They were grateful to the Native Americans for teaching them about native foods. But the Pilgrims missed the taste of English food. Over the years, ships arrived from England with new **colonists** (KOL-un-ists). These colonists brought English meat in the form of cows, pigs, sheep, and chickens.

By the time Benjamin was fifteen years old, his family's land was rich with many English foods, such as peas and apples. His family also grew a few native crops, such as corn and squash.

Benjamin's family had a goat and a cow. Benjamin milked them twice a day and watched his mother make butter from the cream. His mother sold the extra milk to the neighbors.

Everyone had chores to do. Women usually churned the butter and spun thread for making cloth. Men usually chopped the firewood and sharpened tools. ▶

Cooking

Benjamin's mother cooked their food in the huge fireplace in the kitchen. Cooking kettles hung on large hooks and chains that his mother could swing into the fire. She lowered the kettles for boiling, and raised them for cooking things more slowly.

Most Pilgrim meals were boiled. Benjamin's mother put meat and vegetables together in a pot and cooked them until they were soft. Sometimes she baked or grilled meat over the fire. Benjamin liked to turn the meat slowly above the hot coals until it was cooked. The colonists did not like spicy foods, but sometimes they used salt and pepper to flavor their food.

◄ *This is the kitchen of the Whipple family, who lived during the mid-1650s. Most Pilgrim kitchens looked very much like this one.*

Baking

Benjamin's mother baked bread and pies in a thick, heavy iron kettle called a dutch oven. She piled hot coals around and on top of the dutch oven in the fireplace. When she thought the bread or pie was done, she pulled the oven from the coals.

A few years later, Benjamin's father built a real oven with bricks and stones. He built it behind the house so there was no danger of burning their house down. It was Benjamin's job to heat up the oven with hot coals brought from the fireplace. When it was hot, he scraped out the coals. Then his mother put in breads, pies, puddings, meats, and beans with a long, flat shovel called a peel so she wouldn't burn herself.

Pilgrims ate baked goods with almost every meal. ▶

Meats and Vegetables

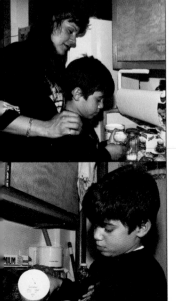

A few years after they arrived in North America, the Pilgrims were eating plenty of their favorite meats—beef, pork, **mutton** (MUT-ten), and chicken. They had no **refrigerators** (ree-FRID-jer-ay-terz), so they salted, pickled, or smoked extra meat to keep it from spoiling. Every fall, Benjamin's mother filled the kitchen shelves with jars of fruits and vegetables. She stored root vegetables, such as carrots, potatoes, onions, and turnips, in a cool root cellar under sand or thick layers of straw. That way they lasted all winter.

New England Mashed Turnips

You will need:

1 pound turnips
½ teaspoon salt
2 tablespoons butter
2 tablespoons half-
   and-half
¼ teaspoon salt
¼ teaspoon ground
   white pepper

This is a tasty dish to eat during the long, winter months.

HOW TO DO IT:

☞ Peel turnips with a vegetable peeler and cut them into ½-inch cubes.
☞ Fill a medium-size pot with water and bring to a boil.
☞ Add ½ teaspoon salt and the turnip cubes and bring to a boil again.
☞ Turn the heat low, cover the pot, and simmer for 20 minutes until the turnips are soft.
☞ Drain the turnips in a colander in the sink.
☞ Put the turnips back into the pot and warm on low heat for a minute to dry off moisture.
☞ Add butter, half-and-half, and the rest of the salt and pepper.
☞ Stir with a spoon while the butter is melting.
☞ Mash with a potato masher until soft and fluffy.

Fruits and Desserts

There were many delicious fruits and berries in North America. But most Pilgrims liked English fruits better. Colonists brought young apple trees from England. The Pilgrims planted apple orchards. Soon they were able to enjoy apples, their favorite English fruit. Later, other colonists brought pear, cherry, plum, and **quince** (KWINTS) trees. All these English fruits grew well in America.

For dessert, and sometimes even for breakfast, Benjamin's mother often made apple pie. She also made apple juice and apple cider for them to drink. And, for the winter, she dried apples, plums, and peaches, and made jellies and jams.

Pilgrims' Honey Apples

You will need:

3 medium or 2 large, tart apples

½ cup honey

2 tablespoons cider vinegar

¼ cup cream

HOW TO DO IT:

☞ Peel, core, and slice each apple into thin slices.

☞ Bring the honey and vinegar to a boil in a medium-size pot.

☞ Turn the heat low and gently place six or eight slices of the apple in the pot at a time.

☞ Simmer about five minutes or until you can see through the slices.

☞ Very carefully scoop out the slices with a slotted spoon.

☞ Spread them on a plate to cool.

☞ Pour cream on top of cooled apples.

This serves four people.

Drinks

Benjamin's family had a cow and a goat, so they could drink fresh milk every day. But Pilgrims had no way to keep milk cold, and warm milk spoils fast. So people who didn't have goats or cows didn't usually drink milk. Most people drank apple juice, apple cider, beer, and water. Benjamin and his father dug wells from which they drank sweet, clean water that they hauled up in buckets.

To help keep warm during winter, Benjamin's mother made tea from the herbs that her Native American neighbors showed her. Sometimes she made a drink that looked, smelled, and tasted kind of like coffee. She made the drink from grains, such as rye and wheat.

Maple-Ginger Tea

You will need:

1 inch piece ginger
1 teaspoon maple
  syrup
1 cup water

HOW TO DO IT:

☞ Boil one cup of water.
☞ Place the ginger in a cup and pour the boiling water over it.
☞ Cover and let the ginger soak for ten minutes.
☞ Scoop out the ginger with a spoon and stir in the maple syrup.
Makes one cup of ginger tea.

The Native Americans taught the Pilgrims how to make this hot tea by using a plant called ginger. The ginger that we buy today comes from a different kind of ginger plant.

Family Meals

Benjamin's family ate their meals together in the kitchen. His mother served each meal in a large wooden bowl that his father had carved. Each person ate from a small wooden bowl with wooden spoons. There were no knives or forks, so the food was cooked in bite-size pieces. A few years later, Benjamin's mother replaced the wooden bowls with pottery made from clay.

Most Pilgrim meals were simple, like the meals many of us eat today. First they ate the main meal with some bread or cornbread and butter. Then they ate a simple dessert. These plain meals were the beginning of basic American cooking.

Glossary

colonist (KOL-un-ist) A person who moves to a new land, but stays under the rule of his or her old country.

harvest (HAR-vest) To gather and bring in crops from the fields.

mutton (MUT-ten) The meat of a sheep.

Pilgrim (PIL-grem) The name of the early English people who settled in North America near what is now Boston, Massachusetts.

quince (KWINTS) A European fruit that looks like a large, yellow apple.

refrigerator (ree-FRID-jer-ay-ter) A machine that is used to make or keep things cold.

settler (SET-ul-er) A person who moves to a new land.

starvation (star-VAY-shun) The point at which lack of food or drink can cause death.

Index